SERIAL KILLERS

John Wayne Gacy

The Killer Clown

by Tom Streissguth

Essential Library
An Imprint of Abdo Publishing
abdobooks.com

ABDOBOOKS.COM

Published by Abdo Publishing, a division of ABDO, PO Box 398166, Minneapolis, Minnesota 55439.

Printed in China.
102024
012025

THIS BOOK CONTAINS RECYCLED MATERIALS

Cover Photo: Bill Waterson/Alamy
Interior Photos: Erin Hooley/Chicago Tribune/Tribune News Service/Getty Images, 4–5, 39, 53, 56, 70, 82; Maine West High School 1978 Yearbook, 7; World History Archive/Alamy, 8; CEK/AP Images, 10, 86–87; Bettmann Archive/Getty Images, 14–15; Shutterstock Images, 17; Barry King/Alamy, 20; Henry Reichel/Chicago History Museum/Archive Photos/Getty Images, 22–23; Bettmann/Getty Images, 24, 76–77, 78; Keith Turrill/Alamy, 29; GHI/Universal History Archive/Universal Images Group/Getty Images, 32–33; William Yates/Chicago Tribune/Tribune News Service/Getty Images, 35, 73; Nam Y. Huh/AP Images, 36; Chicago History Museum, ICHi-176765, 40–41; Rolls Press/Popperfoto/Getty Images, 43; ST-12000839-0001, Chicago Sun-Times Collection, Chicago History Museum, 45; HUM Images/Universal Images Group/Getty Images, 48; Steve Eichner/WireImage/Getty Images, 50–51; ST-19110408-0003, Chicago Sun-Times Collection, Chicago History Museum, 60; Jeffrey Blackler/Alamy, 62–63; Cook County Sheriff's Department/AP Images, 66; Bureau of Prisons/Donaldson Collection/Archive Photos/Getty Images, 75; Charles Bennett/AP Images, 80; Charles Rex Arbogast/AP Images, 85, 99; LES/AP Images, 88, 91; Keri Wiginton/Chicago Tribune/Tribune News Service/Getty Images, 92; Roy Hall/Chicago Tribune/Tribune News Service/Getty Images, 94; Eugene Garcia/AFP/Getty Images, 97

Editor: Marley Richmond
Series Designer: Joshua Olson

Library of Congress Control Number: 2024938307

PUBLISHER'S CATALOGING-IN-PUBLICATION DATA

Names: Streissguth, Tom, author.
Title: John Wayne Gacy: the killer clown / by Tom Streissguth
Other title: the killer clown
Description: Minneapolis, Minnesota: ABDO Publishing, 2025 | Series: Serial killers | Includes online resources and index.
Identifiers: ISBN 9781098295356 (lib. bdg.) | ISBN 9798384916352 (ebook)
Subjects: LCSH: Gacy, John Wayne--Juvenile literature. | Killers (Murderers)--Biographies--Juvenile literature. | Serial killers--Biographies--Juvenile literature. | Crime--Juvenile literature. | True crime stories--Juvenile literature.
Classification: DDC 364.15232--dc23

CONTENTS

This book discusses accounts of crime, violence, and death that may be disturbing to some readers.

CHAPTER 1

A MISSING PERSON

Nisson Pharmacy occupied a one-story brick building along busy Touhy Avenue in the suburban town of Des Plaines, Illinois. On the cold day of December 11, 1978, two young employees were working in the front of the store. Whenever the front door opened and customers came in, a harsh winter wind came in with them. It chilled 17-year-old Kim Byers to the bone.

Kim was working the evening shift. She stood at the cash register, checking through items and taking payments. From time to time, she could spot Rob Piest. Rob was just 15, but he didn't mind stocking shelves part time for a little extra spending money. Kim thought he was a good guy and easy to talk to. On that wintry day, Kim asked to borrow his blue parka so she could warm up a little.

Rob agreed and brought out the coat for Kim to put on. A little more comfortable, Kim went about her job.

Rob's blue parka would eventually be used as evidence in a criminal trial.

On her break, still wearing the coat, she went to the photo counter. She wanted to have some pictures printed as a gift for her sister. The receipt she tore off the top of the photo envelope had a serial number and the name of the pharmacy.

The receipt was just a piece of scrap paper that Kim didn't need. She could easily retrieve her pictures any time without it, since she worked at the store. Kim found a trash can and threw the receipt away. But then a strange impulse came over her. She looked at the receipt, pulled it out of the trash, and put it in the pocket of Rob's coat.

A Stranger in the Store

At about 9:00 p.m. that evening, Rob's mom, Elizabeth, came into Nisson Pharmacy. She was there to drive him home. It was her birthday, and the family was going to celebrate. Rob collected his stuff from the back room, and he got his blue parka from Kim. He told his mom to wait a few minutes. He needed to speak to someone about a construction job.

Kim had seen a man in the store earlier in the day talking to her boss, Phil Torf, about doing some remodeling work for Nisson. To Kim, something about him seemed out of place. "Who's that?" she asked Torf, curious about the man.[1] Torf said the man's name was John Gacy. Kim had never heard of him.

Gacy had left that afternoon, then returned in the evening to retrieve an appointment book he left behind. Rob wanted to speak to him about a potential job before he left. Rob's mom waited. The minutes dragged on, but Rob didn't return to the store. Mrs. Piest checked the parking lot and looked behind the pharmacy. Rob and Gacy were nowhere to be seen.

Rob was a sophomore in high school when he worked at Nisson Pharmacy.

Encounter with a Killer

Gacy pulled into his driveway in a black pickup truck. He and Rob climbed out of the truck and walked inside the house. Rob may have noticed Gacy's odd sense of interior decorating. There were a few potted plants and some heavy furniture. A jagged stripe in several colors decorated a wall in the hallway. And on almost every wall, in every room, hung paintings of clowns.

Rob had noticed that Gacy was a talkative man whose favorite subject was himself. He mentioned connections he had with important people. He described the fun of working for his company, PDM Contractors. He soon got on the topic of clowns. Gacy talked a little bit about his own clown character, Pogo, which he portrayed to entertain people in his free time.

At some point, Gacy offered to show Rob a magic trick. He put himself in a pair of handcuffs, twirled away from the boy, then turned back. His hands, somehow, were free. Rob thought it was an impressive trick, and he agreed when Gacy offered to show him how it was done.

Gacy put the cuffs on Rob. The boy asked how he could escape them. But Gacy said there was only one way to get out of a pair of handcuffs. He asked, "Do you have the key, Rob?"[2]

Gacy stood there, showing Rob the little key that would free him from the handcuffs. Rob stared at the

When he was dressed as Pogo, Gacy painted on a white face with a large, red mouth.

older man, not sure what was happening. The moment stretched on. Then Gacy used the key to free Rob from the cuffs. But soon after, Gacy would show Rob a different trick. In this one, he used a short, sturdy length of rope wrapped around Rob's neck.

WHY POGO?

John Wayne Gacy's fame rests on his career as a serial killer, but he is also known for his clowning. To relax, he would put on a clown outfit, complete with face paint and balloons, and entertain at parties, parades, and other events. His clown character went by the name Pogo. Pogo is a portmanteau, or a combination of words. *Po* stands for "Polish," which was the nationality of Gacy's family, while *Go* comes from the phrase "on the go." Gacy was proud of his hard work as a contractor, and he saw Pogo the clown as Polish and on the go.

Reported Missing

In her car parked in front of Nisson Pharmacy, Elizabeth Piest worried. She didn't think her son would just disappear. He didn't get in trouble, didn't have problems at school, and never threatened to run away. At Maine West High School, he was an honor student. Rob was a good kid and a good son. And now he was gone.

Mrs. Piest drove home and told her family Rob was missing. Her husband, daughter, and other son all piled in to the car, along with their two German shepherds. For a couple of hours, they searched the neighborhood around the pharmacy. When they didn't find Rob, they drove

Elizabeth Piest, *second from right*, was one of the few spectators allowed to attend Gacy's eventual trial.

to the Des Plaines police station, where Elizabeth Piest reported her son missing.

The officer on duty took the report, but it was late at night. People, especially teenagers, often went missing only to return on their own, and at this time of day there was nobody available to follow up on the Piests' report. As a general rule, Des Plaines and other police departments waited 72 hours, or three days, before taking any action on a missing person. The officer laid Rob's file aside, along with the evening's other reports, for the officer on duty in the morning.

The Search

Lieutenant Joseph Kozenczak had been chief of detectives at the Des Plaines Police Department for just six months. His morning routine included going through reports from the previous evening. While reading this paperwork, he turned up the Piest missing persons report.

Kozenczak suspected this report was serious. He decided to overlook the 72-hour rule. He assigned Officer Ron Adams to investigate. Adams got started early. He interviewed the Piest family as well as Phil Torf and others at Nisson Pharmacy. Torf revealed that Gacy had been in the store the evening prior. Adams also paid a visit to Maine West High School. He interviewed Rob's friends and teachers as well as Kim Byers. He got no leads on where the teenager might be.

STRANGER DANGER

Gacy's murder spree during the 1970s helped focus national attention on the issue of disappearing children. In the 1980s, federal and local police began sharing information about missing children. A national computer database of the missing was set up. Schools offered classes and programs about stranger danger, which aimed to help children stay safe around people they didn't know. Ads about missing children ran on television and in other media. The National Center for Missing and Exploited Children was founded in 1984.

Adams also phoned Gacy. It was about 9:30 in the morning. Gacy denied speaking to any kids. "I can't help you," he told Adams. "I don't know anything about it."[3] But Gacy did agree to come down to the Des Plaines police station to give a statement.

Later that day, Gacy appeared at the station. He signed a written statement that said he knew nothing about Rob Piest. Kozenczak and the other police officers observed that Gacy and his car were splashed with mud, as if he had recently been digging. But it was December, and the ground was frozen.

Searching for a Clue

Kozenczak then did some digging of his own. Gacy's home address was close by, in Norwood Park. Gacy ran a contracting company, PDM Construction. He owned a truck, a van, and a 1979 Oldsmobile car. In 1968, he had been arrested and charged with a sexual crime in

PRIOR CHARGES

Lieutenant Kozenczak searched Gacy's police record after he learned the man was one of the last people to see Rob before he disappeared. One entry showed that Gacy had been charged with aggravated battery in 1972. When Kozenczak looked into the complaint, he learned the complainant said Gacy had coerced him into performing sex acts and had later beaten him. Although the charges were eventually dropped, Kozenczak saw this as another piece of evidence pointing to suspicious activity in Rob's case.

Waterloo, Iowa. Found guilty, he had served 18 months of a ten-year sentence before being released on parole.[4]

Kozenczak decided to request a search warrant for Gacy's house. This document would give him legal authority to enter Gacy's property. Knowing that Gacy had crossed paths with Rob Piest the night before, Kozenczak believed he had probable cause to search Gacy's house. Judge Marvin Peters agreed, and he signed the warrant. It was about 3:00 p.m. on December 13, and it was time for the police to pay John Wayne Gacy's home a visit.

CHAPTER 2

GROWING UP GACY

John Wayne Gacy was born in 1942. His parents were John and Marion Gacy, and he had an older and a younger sister. When he was just a kid, John Jr. would often spend time in the garage with his dad. He looked up to John Sr., who was the son of Polish immigrants. John Sr. had fought in World War I (1914–1918) then came home from Europe. He got married and started a family.

The Gacys lived in a middle-class neighborhood on the northwest side of Chicago, Illinois. The family owned a one-story brick house with a windowed attic and a small porch. John Sr. was a skilled machinist who worked in a factory, and his wife was a homemaker.

Anger at Home

To outsiders, the Gacy family seemed entirely normal. But John Sr. had a dark side. He was angry much of the time,

Karen Kuzma (formerly Gacy), *center*, is the youngest Gacy sibling. She was very close to her brother when they were young children.

and he drank a lot. When he got drunk, John Sr. became violent. He took out any frustrations he was feeling on his wife and his family.

John liked to help his father in the garage. But one day, things in the garage went awry for young John. John was just four years old, so he didn't know anything about cars or car parts. The boy mixed up some small car parts, and John Sr. exploded in anger, yelling at his son for a long time. It frightened young John, and he never forgot the experience.

John Sr. often called his son "dumb and stupid," but that was just one way he expressed his opinion of John Jr.[1] John Sr. also believed in physical punishment. He often used a razor strop. This was a long, heavy strip of brown leather, similar to an oversize belt, normally used to sharpen tools.

NAMED FOR A MOVIE STAR

John Gacy Sr. admired typically masculine heroes, especially those he saw in movies. For that reason, he named his only son John Wayne Gacy after the movie star John Wayne. The actor John Wayne was born Marion Morrison. He got his break in 1930, when he was picked out of a movie crew by director Raoul Walsh to act in *The Big Trail*. Walsh changed Morrison's name to something more memorable and, in his opinion, manly. For the rest of his life, John Wayne played courageous figures in war movies and westerns.

While growing up, John often felt this strop on his back. His father whipped him for causing problems, making mistakes, talking back, or being defiant. Sometimes John Sr. would use his fists, swinging at his son for no reason at all. Between the beatings and the criticism, John began to really believe he was, as his father often said, dumb and stupid.

His father had other frightening habits. He often went down into the basement, locked the door, and talked

Studies have shown that parents who drink alcohol often and heavily are more likely to harm their children than those who do not misuse alcohol.

to himself. He drank heavily and would frequently fly into rages during which he would throw things and hit his kids and wife. Still, deep down, the son wanted his father's attention and acceptance.

Blackouts and High School

John had problems besides his abusive father. In school and at home, he often suffered blackouts. He would suddenly fall to the floor and lie there, unconscious. He went to see doctors, but they could not find anything wrong with him. After many years, doctors would learn that he had suffered a blood clot caused by a blow to his head when he was 11. Following this diagnosis, medication eventually resolved the problem.

But in the meantime, John's father had his own opinion. John Sr. didn't think there was anything wrong, and he accused his son of being lazy and faking his blackouts for attention. The blackouts meant that when he graduated, John wouldn't be accepted by the military, which was a common goal for boys his age. John Sr., a military veteran, hated men who he thought of as soft, and he saw his only son as a prime example of this.

During his teenage years, John began to experience romantic and sexual attraction to girls. He also desired physical intimacy with boys, but he was ashamed of these thoughts and didn't have anyone to talk to about how he felt. John knew his father didn't like gay people, and he was afraid his father knew he desired other boys. John Jr. kept his feelings a secret.

Early Adventure

Frustration and shame were common emotions for John, but one day when he was 20, it all got to be too much. His father had taken an important part out of the car that

John Jr. drove. John Sr. wouldn't replace the part until his son paid him back for a loan on the car. Although John Jr. came up with the money, he had reached a breaking point.

Without saying bye to anyone, he climbed into the car, left Chicago, and headed west. He drove all the way to Las Vegas, Nevada. He had a cousin living there, and it seemed as good a place as any to get a new start.

In Las Vegas, John got a job as an ambulance driver for the Palm Mortuary and Memorial Park. When his employer discovered John was still too young to drive ambulances in Nevada, he was reassigned to a role in the mortuary itself. In this new position, he learned how to clean and embalm dead bodies and prepare them for funerals.

At the mortuary, John had no trouble handling the dead. Instead, he found his work fascinating. Since he didn't have anywhere else to stay, he lived in a room

REVELATION

John moved to Las Vegas in search of a cousin who he knew lived in the city. When he arrived, John found her name in the phone book and paid her a visit. He discovered that she was making a good living as a sex worker. She had a daughter and a house, and she seemed happy and comfortable with the course of her life.

John later told an interviewer that meeting his cousin was a revelation. He realized there was more than one way to live, and sex didn't need to be hidden or shameful. It was all quite different from his strict upbringing back in Chicago.

Some accounts say that Gacy would speak to the dead bodies in Palm Mortuary at night.

at the mortuary. He worked the night shift, often alone. His boss eventually became suspicious.

"The dead won't bother you. It's the living you got to worry about."[2]

—John Wayne Gacy on his time working at a mortuary

He heard John Jr. would sometimes undress bodies and fold their clothes next to their caskets. The boss eventually called the police. Although John was never caught in this behavior, he decided it was time to move on from the mortuary and return home. He was soon back on the road, on his way to Chicago.

MORTUARY STORIES

After Gacy's eventual arrest, when the public and the media learned about his crimes, people began telling stories about his life. Some of those stories may be true, but others are probably false. Some people believe that John slept in caskets with dead bodies or even had sex with them during his time at the mortuary. In later interviews, he denied these stories. "I never climbed into a coffin, or anything like that," he said to one interviewer. "That is so . . . ridiculous."[3]

CHAPTER 3

IN BUSINESS AND IMPRISONMENT

It was 1962, and 20-year-old Gacy was back in Chicago. He lived with his family and had little to his name. But after living on his own in Las Vegas, Gacy felt confident in himself and motivated to work hard.

In an effort to get ahead, Gacy enrolled in the Northwestern Business School. He wanted to learn more about business and earn a better living. This school offered a one-year business course. Gacy got through it and graduated.

Gacy then landed a job as a shoe salesman with the Nunn-Bush Shoe Company. He excelled at his new job by using a talent for engaging people, maintaining their attention with small talk, and making them feel important. After a short time working for Nunn-Bush in Chicago, another opportunity presented itself. The company promoted Gacy to store manager and transferred him to the Roberts department store in Springfield, Illinois.

Chicago could be a violent and dangerous city in the 1960s. The city's murder rate rose quickly during the decade.

In addition to being a good salesman, Gacy had a head for business. He traded shoes from his Nunn-Bush store with outside salesmen, and he soon obtained smart new clothes, flashy cuff links, and expensive ties. These helped him look respectable and affluent.

Meeting Marlynn

In 1964, Gacy met a woman who would change his life's direction. Marlynn Myers also worked at the Roberts store. Her father owned several Kentucky Fried

Chicken (KFC) restaurants. The couple quickly fell in love. Gacy and Myers married in September 1964. In 1965, the couple moved to Waterloo, Iowa, where Marlynn's father had a job waiting for his son-in-law. Gacy saw this as another opportunity. He agreed to quit his job with Nunn-Bush and give the restaurant job a try.

Gacy and Myers settled down in Waterloo. They had a son, Michael, in February 1966 and a daughter,

Gacy enjoyed dressing the part of a boss. He wanted to be an important man whom people respected.

Christine, in March 1967. At KFC, Gacy proved to be a good restaurant manager. Although he didn't always get along with his demanding father-in-law, he strove to make his life and his marriage a success.

Gacy was ambitious and hardworking. He was also good at making connections. He joined the Waterloo chapter of the United States Junior Chamber, or the Jaycees. The Jaycees is a service organization that helps with community events and projects, such as parades and fundraisers. In the Jaycees, Gacy could also network with business leaders.

Gacy rose in the ranks of the Jaycees by making himself useful and volunteering as much as he could. He loved to have dinners, parties, and get-togethers with the other members, many of whom became close personal friends. The organization promoted him to vice president, and in that role he won the honor of Outstanding Vice President of the Year. Gacy soon began planning a run for the Jaycees chapter president.

Trouble in Waterloo

Gacy had a good life in Waterloo, and the future looked bright. He was making good money as a restaurant manager, and he rose quickly in the volunteer organizations he had joined. But at work and in the Jaycees, trouble was brewing.

In 1968, Donald Voorhees, a teenage boy, accused Gacy of sexually assaulting him the year prior. Donald described the incident to his father, who was also a member of the local Jaycees chapter. Voorhees then told the police, who began an investigation. Gacy was arrested and brought to the county jail.

The arrest shocked Gacy's friends and family. They wondered how a good family man and community leader like John Wayne Gacy could be guilty of a sex crime. But Gacy had a simple explanation: he had been framed by the police. To anyone who would listen, he proclaimed his innocence. The whole thing, he explained, was a conspiracy to prevent him from becoming the Jaycees' president.

But Gacy couldn't prove that in court. More than one witness came forward, stating that Gacy had formed a little circle of young men and boys who worked in his restaurants and did odd jobs. He would invite them to his house, offer them liquor, and then proposition them for sex.

A young teenager named Edward Lynch, one of Gacy's employees, said Gacy had assaulted him in late 1967. Gacy had brought the boy home and given him whiskey, then tried to persuade him to perform oral sex. When Edward refused, Gacy forced him into a bedroom at knifepoint. He wrapped chains around the boy and then began choking him. Eventually Edward lost consciousness. Gacy unchained him and then let him go.

INTIMIDATING A WITNESS

Gacy did his best to keep Donald Voorhees from testifying at his trial. Gacy bribed one of his employees, high schooler Russell Schroeder, to attack Donald. In September 1968, Schroeder got Donald alone and began to assault him, throwing punches and spraying mace in his eyes. Donald escaped and ignored Schroeder's threats about going to the police. Schroeder was arrested, and Gacy faced additional charges related to the attack.

The jury found Gacy guilty of sodomy after listening to victims' testimonies. The court also ordered psychiatric evaluations of Gacy. One of the doctors wrote, "The most striking of the test results is the patient's total denial of responsibility for anything that has happened to him. He can produce an 'alibi' for everything."[1] Another labeled Gacy a sexual predator and recommended a harsh sentence.

On December 3, 1968, Gacy was convicted. The court sentenced him to ten years of imprisonment.[2] Gacy was sent to the Anamosa State Reformatory.

Gacy's world fell apart on that day. In another room of the courthouse where the jury announced its verdict, Gacy's wife, Marlynn, was filing for divorce. She stated in her divorce petition that Gacy had subjected her to cruel and inhumane treatment. Because Gacy was going to prison and the couple's marriage was ending, Marlynn also received custody of the couple's two children. Gacy would never see his children again.

THE VANISHING GACYS

After his conviction in Iowa, Gacy lost touch with his family. Marlynn Myers and their kids, Michael and Christine, disappeared from his life. It is likely that all three changed their last name at some point, since reporters have never been able to locate the family. Although Gacy's sister, Karen, sent gifts when the children were young, the gifts were always returned. Karen has given interviews to the media, but no trace of Gacy's first wife or children turned up.

A Prison Success Story

The Anamosa Reformatory was a sprawling stone complex not far from the city of Cedar Rapids, Iowa. Gacy quickly learned that in prison, making connections was still the way to get ahead. He made himself useful, just as he did in Waterloo. Gacy formed a prison chapter of the Jaycees. He also worked his way up to a job as head cook in the kitchen.

Anamosa is a medium- to maximum-security facility. It offers job training and counseling to help inmates succeed after their release.

As a cook, Gacy had one of the prison's key jobs. He had control over the food other inmates received. He might give a friend or an ally a bigger helping. An enemy, or anyone who had crossed Gacy, might get bugs or something else in his soup. People knew Gacy decided how their meals went that day.

Gacy also worked to earn favors and help from the prison officials. He was one of the few prisoners who was free to dress how he wanted. Gacy wore a crisp white button-down shirt, in contrast to other inmates who wore dingy prison clothes.

Gacy applied for parole after serving just five months of his sentence. He said he planned to move to Chicago and live with his mother. The parole board turned him down but said it would reconsider his case in the next year.

Then, just before Christmas in 1969, Gacy's father passed away. Gacy asked for a temporary release to attend the funeral. Although Anamosa officials could temporarily release prisoners, they turned down Gacy's request.

For the rest of his life, Gacy would suffer regret and guilt over not attending the funeral. Gacy knew the low opinion his father had for him. He would always believe that his conviction, along with the shame it brought to the family, had driven his father to an early grave.

In 1970, Gacy managed to convince the parole board he was worth the risk of a one-year parole. In their reports,

A GACY MONUMENT IN IOWA

While at the Anamosa Reformatory, Gacy became what prison officials considered a model prisoner. Not only did he stick to the prison rules but he also kept himself busy and useful. It was at Anamosa that Gacy's career as a contractor began. He persuaded prison officials to let him design a miniature golf course. He built the course in the prison courtyard. It was a big hit with prisoners seeking to pass the time in the fresh air. The Gacy mini golf course is still standing and in use at Anamosa.

the prison administrators wrote that Gacy "would very likely not be involved in the same type of offense as he is presently incarcerated for."[3] He was released from Anamosa in June after serving about 18 months of his ten-year sentence. By the terms of his parole, Gacy would be moving back to the Chicago area and would stay with his mother. If he stayed out of trouble, the court could end his sentence and parole period early.

"When I went through the psychiatric evaluation at Iowa City, I was told I had an antisocial personality. . . . The whole thing was stupid."[4]

—John Wayne Gacy on his time at Anamosa

Gacy's conviction completely transformed his comfortable, middle-class family life. His time in the Jaycees was done, and the friends and family he knew in Waterloo avoided him. But the parole meant he would have a chance at a new start in Chicago.

CHAPTER 4

FIRST VICTIM

After his release from Anamosa Reformatory, Gacy moved in with his mother. Drawing on his experience as a cook at Anamosa, he landed a job at Bruno's, a downtown restaurant and bar. Bruno's was a popular hangout for professional hockey players from the Chicago Blackhawks. With a police station nearby, there were also a lot of cops stopping in for off-duty drinks and relaxation.

Gacy held a certain admiration for law enforcement officers. Citizens respected them, by and large, while criminals feared them. They represented justice, law, and order.

One cop Gacy got to know well was James Hanley. When Hanley came in to Bruno's, he and Gacy would banter and chat. Curious about police work, Gacy liked to ask questions about Hanley's job. Secretly, he wanted to join the force. He owned several police badges and had a

Gacy frequented various bars in Chicago. At least one tavern in the city still boasts that Gacy was a regular customer.

rotating, flashing light he would sometimes place on the roof of his car.

Later on, after Gacy left the kitchen job at Bruno's, he would sometimes call himself Jack Hanley. Jack was Gacy's alter ego, a second personality that Gacy would assume from time to time. Gacy's Jack was a cop, too. It was a personality he used to impress others that allowed him to escape his ordinary life. In the guise of Jack Hanley, he could do things that the ordinary John Wayne Gacy wouldn't or couldn't do.

THE GOOD NEIGHBOR

Gacy's appearance as a successful contractor and engaged community member added a layer of fear to the story of his crimes. While many serial killers are reclusive, Gacy was sociable. He hosted annual summer picnics in the backyard of his house. Gacy would announce the theme, and hundreds of his friends and neighbors showed up in costume. One of Gacy's neighbors said he was "better than a neighbor, he was a good friend."[1] Few people suspected that Gacy was anything other than a good person.

Another Arrest

In 1971, Gacy and his mother bought a house on West Summerdale Avenue in Norwood Park, part of Cook County in Chicago's suburbs. There were two bedrooms, a half-circle driveway in front, and a room that Gacy turned into an office. Instead of a basement, the house had a dark crawl space underneath the main floor. There was nothing down there but wooden supports and joists, some pipes, and a dirt floor.

Gacy's life was returning to normal, but he hadn't been reformed by his short stay in Anamosa. The same desires that had sent Gacy to prison were still there, and his life as a criminal and pedophile resumed in Chicago. In February 1971, Gacy was arrested. A teenage boy had accused Gacy of rape.

When the victim failed to show up for Gacy's trial, the case was dropped. Without a witness to testify to a crime, and with no physical evidence, there was nothing to prove

The Gacys' house was outside Chicago's city limits. The Chicago Police Department did not have authority in this area, which made it more difficult to build a case against Gacy.

it had actually happened. It was Gacy's word against that of his accuser. Gacy's parole officer never found out about the charge.

Cruising Downtown

Like his father, Gacy was good with his hands. He could wield tools, build things, and make repairs. He knew how houses were constructed, and he was a skilled painter and remodeler. He decided to put these talents to work and start his own business. He named it PDM Contractors, for Painting, Decorating, and Maintenance.

With Gacy's gift for making connections and selling himself, the little company did well. PDM took up a lot

Intercity buses are one way for people to travel across North America. However, starting in the 1970s, buses and bus stations became known as dangerous and dirty places.

of Gacy's time. But he had the energy for it.

In fact, Gacy didn't sleep much. At night, after a day's work, he would get into his car and cruise Chicago's busy freeways downtown. He would drive around the city blocks, looking for men and boys to bring home. One of his favorite areas was the bustling downtown Greyhound bus station.

GACY'S SEXUALITY

When Gacy picked up boys and young men, he often brought them back to his home and paid them for sex. Gacy claimed that he did not attack his victims unless something went wrong. If a victim raised his price for the encounter, or if he expressed regret after the sexual act, Gacy turned violent. Although he engaged in sex with men, Gacy expressed to others a deep hatred of gay people. Some experts say feelings of guilt and shame surrounding his sexuality may have played into Gacy's crimes.

People leaving and arriving wandered the streets near the bus station. Some of them were there for a few hours, waiting for their transportation. Others didn't have homes and lived on the streets. A few were runaways, teenagers, or young men in need of money. Gacy spoke to these people frequently while sitting in his parked car. They became his targets, and, later, his victims.

On January 3, 1972, while driving alone downtown, Gacy came across Tim McCoy, a 16-year-old from Nebraska who was on his way home from a trip to visit family in Michigan. Gacy offered to show Tim a few Chicago sights. Then he invited the boy out to his house in Norwood Park. That night, Tim decided to miss his bus and stay at the Gacy house. Marion Gacy was away, staying with her sister. She would not be home for a few days.

REMEMBERING TIM McCOY

A few years before Tim McCoy's death, his parents divorced. Tim didn't like his new stepfather, which was one of his reasons for traveling the country on foot and by bus. However, Tim spent much time with his aunts, uncles, and cousins, whom he visited for Christmas in 1971 before boarding a bus to Chicago. "Tim was one of [those] guys that, when you were around him, he was happy," said his cousin. "He'd make you laugh."[2] Tim promised to call his family after his trip to Chicago, but the call never came.

The Death of Tim McCoy

Gacy later said that he and Tim had sex that night. Gacy claims that the encounter was consensual. Afterward, the pair fell asleep.

In Gacy's account, he woke up in the morning to Tim standing in the doorway with a knife. Fearing for his life, Gacy began struggling with the teenage boy. In the narrow hallway, there was little room to maneuver. Gacy felt that he had no way to escape. He stabbed Tim in the chest, and the boy fell to the floor.

The entrance to Gacy's crawl space would eventually be removed from his home. It was displayed in the courtroom during his trial.

Tim lived for a few minutes, but he soon stopped breathing. Gacy tried to figure out what to do. It was morning, and daylight streamed through the windows of the house. To Gacy, it may not have seemed safe to move the body around outside during the day. So Gacy decided to climb the attic stairs and keep Tim's corpse under the house rafters.

Eventually Gacy would move Tim's body down to the house's crawl space and bury it. There was plenty of room down there for a hidden, makeshift grave. The floor was dirt, and the crawl space was unfinished. The only way to access the space was through a trapdoor in the floor of a closet. It seemed a perfect hiding place for just about anything—one Gacy could use and forget. Tim McCoy was Gacy's first murder victim, but he wouldn't be the last. Gacy had begun his career as a serial killer.

CHAPTER 5

AN UPSTANDING CITIZEN

Carole Hoff was an old friend and classmate of Gacy's sister, Karen. Hoff and Gacy had been friends when they were younger, and they had once gone on a date together. In 1971, they resumed their friendship. After a short time, they grew close. Hoff was divorced by this time and had two young daughters of her own.

The couple got to know each other better over the next few months. Gacy explained to Hoff that he was bisexual. That meant he enjoyed physical intimacy with men as well as women. Hoff didn't quite understand Gacy's sexuality, but it wasn't that important

Law enforcement experts say that many serial killers appear to be normal members of the community. This is one reason they are difficult to catch.

PUBLIC SERVANT

When he was not leading his murderous second life, Gacy was civic minded, and no public service job was too unimportant for him. In 1975, he accepted an appointment as the secretary-treasurer of the Norwood Park Township Street Lighting District. The job called for him to keep the financial books for the district and take care of the neighborhood's public streetlights. He came up with a system of putting numbers on individual streetlights that made it easier for residents to identify any that weren't working.

to her. He was gentle with her daughters, and she thought he was a good man.

In the summer of 1972, Gacy and Hoff married. Hoff and her two girls moved in to the house on West Summerdale Avenue, where Gacy had already buried his first victim. John's mother, Marion Gacy, believed two families living together was a bad idea, so she moved out of the house and into her own apartment.

Once again, Gacy acted the part of a family man with a wife and kids to support. But his job at Bruno's was taking time Gacy needed for his contracting business. In 1973, he quit that job and went full-time as a self-employed contractor.

Gacy kept busy day and night with the business. He spent any free time in his backyard and garage, puttering and fixing things. Over time, the garage turned into his private sanctuary where Hoff and the girls weren't supposed to go.

Precinct Captain

Gacy was still striving for more. He used personal connections to get ahead. He joined the Democratic Party, which dominated politics and government in Chicago. The party would eventually make him a precinct captain of Norwood Park. In this position, his job was to represent the party, do good work in the community, and help increase voter turnout at election time.

Precinct captains earned no salary in their roles. They were volunteers who donated their time to the party. But for Gacy, the position still brought something valuable: influential friends. He met officials who held real power,

Many important Democratic Party rallies took place in Chicago during the 1970s.

including city council members, police heads, and mayors. Gacy was certain these connections could help him build his own political career.

A Second Killing

A busy contractor needs employees, and Gacy had no trouble finding them. Young men and teenagers were eager for well-paying jobs, and Gacy paid well. For them, working for PDM was a good way to gain work experience. For Gacy, hiring young employees was also a way to find sexual partners.

John Butkovich was one of Gacy's teenage recruits. He started working for PDM in 1974. He had dropped out of Lane Technical High School and was working in a hardware store when he met Gacy. By that time, PDM was getting busy with remodeling jobs. Instead of a dropout, Gacy saw a young man who was eager to work, and Butkovich agreed to take the open position.

"I wanted to go for mayor. . . . If that worked, I was going to run for the state senate. I didn't see any limits."[1]

—John Wayne Gacy on his political aspirations

Butkovich and Gacy got along. Gacy would sometimes invite the boy over after work. On a few late nights, Butkovich stayed overnight. But he didn't last very long

Butkovich, *top right*, had five siblings. His father thought Gacy was a good man when Butkovich worked for him.

with PDM. He quit the job after eight months. At this point, Gacy still owed him money. The last paycheck never arrived.

Butkovich let it go until July 31, 1975. Finally, he realized he would have to ask for his last two weeks' pay with a little more force. So he asked a friend of his to go with him to Gacy's house. The friend agreed.

At the house, Gacy and Butkovich argued. Gacy brought up the subject of materials he had let Butkovich borrow from PDM. There would be no last paycheck. In fact, Gacy said, Butkovich owed money to Gacy.

Eventually both men calmed down. Butkovich took his friend home. Later that night, Gacy ran into Butkovich in Uptown Chicago, and their argument resumed. Gacy tried to calm down his former employee, so he brought Butkovich back to Norwood Park and then offered him liquor. Now a little bit drunk, and no longer angry, Butkovich agreed to let Gacy try a magic trick.

SEARCHING FOR JOHN BUTKOVICH

After John Butkovich went missing, his father, Marco, found the boy's car parked on the street with the keys inside. Marco thought this was strange, so he called the police. Officers came to investigate the car, and Marco told them his son had planned to confront Gacy the previous night. When interviewed by the officers, Gacy said he had argued with Butkovich at the house, then the boy and his friend had left. Without any additional evidence, the officers believed Butkovich had simply run away. The Butkovich family regularly called the police for years, but nothing more was done to find their son.

Gacy put a pair of handcuffs on Butkovich, then challenged him to get free. As Butkovich struggled, Gacy strangled him. He took the young man's body out to his garage and buried it in a hole he had dug for a well.

It had been three and a half years since the murder of Tim McCoy. Killing John Butkovich, however, would set Gacy off on a murder spree that lasted six and a half years. During this time, more than 30 of Gacy's victims vanished from their homes and families—all of them dying the same way as John Butkovich.[2]

Man About Town

Carole Hoff grew increasingly unhappy in her marriage to Gacy. Her husband was frequently away from home, even in the late evenings, and sometimes all night long. When she asked him what he was up to, his answer was always the same: business. He claimed to have meetings with partners, customers, and prospective clients that could take place any time of the day or night.

It also seemed strange to Hoff that Gacy spent so much time in the garage, which lay a few yards east of the house. Gacy would disappear in there, behind locked doors, just as his own father used to disappear into a locked basement room. When Hoff asked what he was doing, Gacy just brushed it off. One day, when she had a chance to peek inside the garage, Hoff found a mattress on the floor.

NOT JUST THE PAST

The house on West Summerdale Avenue was Gacy's home, and it was where he murdered many victims. It remains a place of fascination for crime tourists and other curious visitors. Even though the Gacy residence was torn down more than 40 years ago, people arrive to look and take pictures. A new home was built on the empty lot in 1988. The street number was changed so that no trace of Gacy's residence survives. In 1991, the home's owner was interviewed by a newspaper reporter. "The past is the past. . . . This is just a house now," he said.[3]

Teenagers in Uptown Chicago told police that a man named John was regularly picking up young men in the area. But nothing came of the reports.

In fact, Gacy had an entirely separate existence from his life as a family man, a father to two girls, and a business owner. He was keeping up his nighttime cruising, when he would drive the Chicago streets looking for men, boys, and sex. He frequented the streets around the Greyhound bus station, as well as the Uptown neighborhood and Washington Square Park, also known as Bughouse Square. He would pick up pedestrians, sometimes claiming to be a police officer. He would drive them around and sometimes bring them back to his garage.

By late 1975, Hoff and Gacy were growing apart. Their arguments became more frequent. They fought about money and Gacy's late-night disappearances. Hoff had offered to help Gacy as an accountant, but she simply didn't know how to handle the business's financial records.

Eventually Gacy had to straighten out the company finances himself, which led to more of his angry outbursts. These outbursts were getting frequent, and Hoff had reached her limit. In March 1976, Hoff and Gacy divorced. Hoff and her daughters moved out of the house.

CHAPTER 6

THE SUSPECT

John Wayne Gacy amused kids and families around Chicago as Pogo the clown. Gacy created the character himself, including the colorful face, the billowy clown clothes, and the silly hat. He dressed up as Pogo to march in parades, visit kids' birthday parties, entertain at fundraisers, and have fun with friends at backyard barbecues. He grew skilled at doing funny bits and magic tricks he learned from watching other clowns.

Gacy was no longer in the Jaycees, but he did join a community group called the Fraternal Order of Moose. In 1975, he signed up with a Moose group known as the Jolly Joker Clown Club. Soon Gacy was dressing up as Pogo for any occasion that called for a clown. After a time, he felt comfortable enough in the outfit to keep it on after a performance. From time to time, he showed up at The Good Luck Lounge, his favorite Chicago hangout, while wearing his Pogo garb.

Gacy painted portraits of himself as Pogo the clown. He first designed the makeup for his character while serving time at Anamosa.

For Gacy, acting as a clown was also a good way to get away with inappropriate actions. He would step on people's feet, squeeze their noses, and run his hands over the front of women's shirts. To Gacy, being a clown was about deception, or being somebody else. "When you clowned, you're hiding your image," Gacy said. "There are things you could do [as a clown] that you wouldn't do as a person."[1]

"Clowns can get away with anything. . . . Clowns can get away with murder."[2]

—John Wayne Gacy in an interview

Pogo's specialties were sleight of hand and magic tricks. One of his tricks involved handcuffs. He would slip a pair of cuffs around his own wrists behind his back, after secretly hiding a key in one of his sleeves. Retrieving the key, he opened the cuffs out of sight. If he did the trick right, it looked like magic.

The Handcuff Trick

At the same time he was running a contracting business and dressing up as Pogo the clown, Gacy kept up his nighttime cruising in Chicago. He drove to the Uptown neighborhood or Bughouse Square, places where young men met each other. He offered these men a ride or drugs.

He brought some men home to his place, usually for sex. Some spent a few hours in his house and then got a ride home or back to downtown Chicago. Those who resisted Gacy, or who threatened him in any way, risked their lives.

BAD MAKEUP

Professional clowns say Gacy didn't follow tradition when designing Pogo's face. Clowns know they can be frightening to children, so they try to design makeup that is funny and non-threatening. Most clowns draw rounded outlines around their mouths and eyes. Gacy's sharp-cornered mouth and eye outlines went against this rule. He may not have been aware of the tradition, or he may not have cared. This odd makeup is one reason that photographs of Pogo appear so strange and unsettling.

Police found a rope that Gacy used to strangle his victims. It was used as evidence in his trial.

Starting with John Butkovich, Gacy used his handcuff trick to carry out murder. The victim was invited to try the handcuffs, then Gacy withheld the key. For those he decided to kill, Gacy used a length of rope and a short wooden stick.

He circled the neck of his handcuffed victim with the rope. He then inserted a wooden stick in a loop behind the victim's head. By twisting the stick, he tightened the rope and strangled the victim. Unable to move or breathe, victims panicked and flailed. The rope grew even tighter, and death came quickly. This was the method Gacy used to kill all of his victims except the first, Tim McCoy.

Gacy was an opportunistic killer who didn't plan his murders in advance. He encountered several of his victims, such as John Butkovich, as employees of his contracting business. Others were chance meetings in Chicago's Uptown neighborhood. Rick Johnston, another of Gacy's victims, left a concert on the evening of August 6, 1976, and disappeared. He may have accepted a ride Gacy offered while Gacy was cruising the neighborhood in his car.

Gacy also developed a routine for disposing of the bodies. He brought them down into the crawl space beneath his house and buried them in shallow graves. Gacy dug some of the graves himself, and others were dug by employees he sent into the crawl space with specific directions on where and how deep to dig. He told these employees that he needed shallow trenches in order to lay pipe for one project or another.

Gacy seemed to pick up the pace of his killings in 1976. Approximately 15 of his eventual victims went missing that year.[3] The men he met cruising, along with his employees, were all potential victims. Most of Gacy's workers saw him as a generous and hardworking boss.

He had plenty of work for them, and he paid well. But if one of Gacy's workers gave him any trouble, especially over money, they risked being marked for murder. Gacy also didn't like anyone threatening to reveal his sexual activities. In response, he would threaten to have them murdered or kill them himself.

JUST A COINCIDENCE?

Stephen King's novel *It* was published in 1986, years after John Wayne Gacy's crimes were discovered. The book introduced Pennywise, a supernatural killer clown. Every 27 years, Pennywise appears in his terrifying getup to murder random children in Derry, Maine. Many people have guessed that Gacy was the inspiration for Pennywise. King has never said as much. Instead, he claims that as a horror author, he was just looking for a figure that children and many adults are naturally afraid of.

Trouble with the Cops

Over the years since his arrival back in Chicago, Gacy had drawn attention from the police. On one occasion, in January 1976, he became a suspect in the disappearance of a nine-year-old boy, John Ferris. Gacy was known to cruise in the area where John Ferris lived. Investigators decided to run a stakeout on Gacy's house in Norwood Park.

During the stakeout, officers spent many hours in a car, watching Gacy's house. From time to time, men and boys entered or left the residence. The police stopped and

Gacy's handcuffs would become one of the first pieces of evidence law enforcement officers found that tied him to the disappearances under investigation.

questioned some of the men. The visitors said little. After a few weeks, the police ended the surveillance. They hadn't learned anything that would reveal the whereabouts of John Ferris. A few months later, the boy turned up alive. Gacy was never linked to his disappearance.

Bringing Charges

Nothing came of the police investigation into Gacy in 1976, but Gacy's crimes continued and evidence against him mounted. On December 30, 1977, 19-year-old Robert Donnelly was standing at a bus stop in northwest Chicago when Gacy pulled up in his black Oldsmobile. Gacy pulled out a gun and told Donnelly to get in the car.

Donnelly assumed Gacy was a police officer. With a gun pointed at him, the young man had no choice but to comply. Gacy then drove Donnelly out to his house in Norwood Park, where he put Donnelly into handcuffs and spent several hours raping and torturing him.

Gacy repeatedly forced Donnelly's head into a bathtub full of water, and Donnelly lost consciousness several times. At one point, the young man was forced to watch helplessly as Gacy played Russian roulette with a pistol. This is a game of chance where someone spins a revolver loaded with only one bullet, then shoots. Gacy aimed the gun at Donnelly's head and continued to pull the trigger until finally, a shot rang out. But it was only a blank, which made a loud noise but did not shoot a bullet.

Finally, Gacy put Donnelly, who was still handcuffed, back in his car. Telling Donnelly to get down on the floor, Gacy drove downtown, where he let his victim go. "If you go to the cops, I'll hunt you down," Gacy said. "The cops won't believe you anyway."[4] Before Gacy pulled away from the curb, Donnelly got a good look at the license plate. He remembered its number.

Donnelly then went to his uncle's house, where he was advised to go to the police. The police at the 20th District station took his information, including Gacy's plate number, then sent Donnelly to the hospital. On January 6, 1978, Gacy was arrested at his home and charged with deviate sexual conduct. An assistant state's attorney interviewed Gacy, who admitted that he had taken Donnelly home and had sex with him. But he claimed he had not used force or threatened the man. Gacy said Donnelly had been a willing participant in their sexual acts.

The problem with this case was the same as with other complaints against Gacy. Investigators heard two conflicting stories—one from a teenager, and the other from an adult who was a homeowner, a self-made businessman, and a pillar of the community. Police found no evidence of wrongdoing, except for Donnelly's injuries. But Gacy said those had been a consensual part of their encounter. The assistant state's attorney dropped the charges.

Another Discounted Report

Something similar happened to Jeffrey Rignall on March 21, 1978. While Rignall was walking down a sidewalk in the northwest Chicago suburb of Rosemont, Gacy approached in his car. Through the window, Gacy offered marijuana and a ride, which Rignall accepted. Once Rignall was in the passenger seat, Gacy placed a chloroformed cloth over his face. The chloroform instantly knocked Rignall unconscious.

Waking up later in Gacy's house, Rignall found himself chained to a length of wood. Gacy proceeded to rape and torture Rignall for several hours. In his moments of consciousness, Rignall spotted another man in the room, who didn't speak or identify himself.

The next morning, Gacy drove the still-unconscious Rignall to Lincoln Park in downtown Chicago, where he

FIRST LADY PHOTO OP

In 1978, Gacy was appointed as a leader of the Polish Constitution Day Parade in Chicago. A private reception was held for parade leaders and local politicians. First Lady Rosalynn Carter, wife of President Jimmy Carter, attended. At one point, Gacy and Carter posed together for a photograph. The photo later caused a stir with the Secret Service, which is tasked with protecting the presidential family. In the photo, Gacy wears a pin showing he had been investigated and cleared to meet the First Lady. After Gacy's crimes came to light, the public criticized the Secret Service for having cleared Gacy that day.

Rignall wrote a book about his experience with Gacy titled *29 Below*.

dumped Rignall under a statue of Alexander Hamilton. Rignall went to the hospital, where police came to interview him. But the police did not take Rignall's story seriously. Rignall believed the police discarded his accusation against Gacy because Rignall was gay.

Unable to convince the police, Rignall decided to investigate on his own. He recalled seeing a freeway exit sign for Cumberland Avenue while Gacy was driving. Rignall found a Cumberland Avenue exit on Interstate 90, nearby O'Hare Airport. Staking out the streets nearby, he spent a month waiting to spot Gacy's black Oldsmobile. When it finally showed up, Rignall followed the car, took down the license plate number, then went to the police to turn over the information.

The police quickly tracked down the license plate. A state's attorney then filed a charge against Gacy, this time for battery. But facing another uncertain conclusion, and with little solid evidence to go on, the police allowed Gacy to go free. Rignall's complaint against Gacy was still open when Rob Piest disappeared on the night of December 11, 1978.

CHAPTER 7

THE CHASE

After the disappearance of Rob Piest, Nisson Pharmacy became an unofficial search headquarters. Family and friends of the teenager gathered to plan and organize. Some volunteered to search for Rob. Others passed out flyers showing pictures of the missing boy. Des Plaines police were also keeping eyes on the pharmacy. The cops took statements from people who either knew Rob or had seen him the night he disappeared.

Lieutenant Joseph Kozenczak called John Wayne Gacy on December 12. The lieutenant asked Gacy to come down to the station, answer some questions, and sign a statement. Gacy agreed, but he took his time making it to the station. First, Gacy knew he had an important job to do, and it had to be done immediately. He pulled Rob's body down from his attic, placed it in the trunk of his car, then drove south on Interstate 55.

Posters showing a missing person are one tool to help locate the person.

Arriving at a bridge over the Des Plaines River, Gacy stopped, opened the trunk, and pulled the body out. He then dropped it into the river. Gacy drove back north and arrived at the Des Plaines police station in the early morning hours of December 13. He found that Kozenczak had already left, so Gacy drove home. He returned to the station later that morning.

By this time, Kozenczak was convinced that Gacy knew something about Rob's disappearance. But the lieutenant had to act fast and not give Gacy a chance to hide or

TROUBLE WITH WARRANTS

The search warrants Des Plaines detectives executed on Gacy's house became a legal issue in the case. Warrants require police to have probable cause. This means that there is enough evidence for police to believe a particular crime has taken place.

Lieutenant Kozenczak did not provide specific probable cause in the warrant he prepared to search Gacy's home. Kozenczak didn't yet know if Rob Piest was the victim of a kidnapping, assault, sexual crime, or murder. Gacy's lawyers would later argue that the search warrant was not legitimate because of this missing information.

get rid of any incriminating evidence. Kozenczak wrote up a search warrant. A warrant allows the police to search private property, such as a house, if they suspect a crime has taken place. That afternoon, Kozenczak brought the warrant to Judge Marvin Peters, who made it official by signing it.

Kozenczak's interview with Gacy that morning didn't accomplish much. Gacy denied talking to Rob or any other young people at the pharmacy. Kozenczak then told Gacy that the police were about to search his home.

The lieutenant asked for the keys to the house. Gacy refused to turn them over. Kozenczak then told Gacy that if he didn't turn over the keys, police would tear down the front door. Angered, Gacy tossed his keys on the floor for the cops to retrieve. Kozenczak later described Gacy, saying, "He was a belligerent personality. He wanted to be in control all the time."[1] In that moment, Gacy had lost control.

Searching a House of Death

Later that day, a team of police detectives walked carefully through Gacy's house on West Summerdale Avenue. During the search, Lieutenant Kozenczak found a photo receipt from Nisson Pharmacy. There was no name on the receipt, so he didn't know whose it was, but he kept the receipt as possible evidence. The police also found a section of blood-stained carpet, a rope, and a set of handcuffs. There were driver's licenses and wallets that didn't belong to Gacy. Searchers also found a high school class ring with the initials JAS.

Investigators soon discovered the crawl space trapdoor in the floor of a hall closet. Detective Rafael Tovar

MISSING EVIDENCE

It's standard practice for police departments to keep evidence used in criminal trials. Evidence in Gacy's trial included items that belonged to his victims as well as Gacy's two clown suits, one red and one white. At some point, these suits disappeared from the evidence room in Chicago where they were stored. According to one account, they were sold by a Chicago public employee for $25,000.[2] After this sale, the trail went cold until another collector donated them to the National Crime Museum, which is now part of the Alcatraz East attraction in Pigeon Forge, Tennessee.

volunteered to go into the crawl space and have a look. Using his flashlight, Tovar made his way slowly, his upper body bent to fit through the crawl space. He found a dark and dank space, with an uneven floor of earth, running the entire length of the house. There was lime scattered here and there, which is a material used in construction to keep soil dry and stable. But there was nothing else to see.

Investigators separated remains and other evidence eventually found under Gacy's crawl space into buckets.

The search did turn up some circumstantial evidence. In a criminal investigation, this is indirect evidence that gives investigators reason to suspect that a crime has occurred. But nothing could yet prove that Gacy was guilty of either murder or kidnapping. Although he didn't have much to go on, Kozenczak ordered 24-hour surveillance of Gacy.

Wherever he went, and whatever he did, Gacy would now have members of the Delta Unit, a Des Plaines police squad in charge of surveillance, following him. Four detectives would take part. They worked in two-man teams, with each following Gacy for 12 hours at a stretch.[3]

Cat and Mouse

Gacy was not an easy target for surveillance. He kept up a busy schedule of meetings and appointments. In the evenings, he dropped in to restaurants and bars. After getting home in the middle of the night, he would sleep for a few hours before getting up and starting his busy routine all over again.

Racing through Chicago in his black Oldsmobile, Gacy paid no attention to speed limits or traffic laws. He sped down icy side streets and commercial drags at 40 to 50 miles per hour (64–80 kmh).[4] On the busy freeways that lace through the city, he floored it whenever traffic allowed.

There was nothing secret about the surveillance. Gacy knew he was being followed. Instead of trying to lose the cops, he decided to make the best of it and make friends with his watchers. He would sometimes invite the officers into his house or tell them where he was going. On Sunday, December 17, after spending a few hours at a job site, he went home to get his bowling ball. Before leaving, he informed the police that he had league play that evening.

Pulling up to restaurants and bars that he knew, Gacy invited his pursuers in to share a meal or a drink. He introduced them to the other patrons as his bodyguards. Everywhere he went, the police noted, he seemed to know a lot of people on a first-name basis. Gacy was a popular man.

Late-Night Confession

The surveillance continued and eventually began to wear Gacy down. He had grown tired of police constantly following him in unmarked cars. The police had seized two of Gacy's vehicles and searched his home. It was harassment, in his view, and he intended to do something about it. He contacted a lawyer, Sam Amirante, whom he knew through his contacts with local police, lawyers, and court staff. Amirante had served five years as a public defender in Chicago, representing people accused of crimes but without the money for a lawyer. He had just gone into private practice, and Gacy would be his first client.

Listening to Gacy, Amirante decided that he needed to stop the harassment. He prepared a complaint and a motion for an emergency hearing. The court set the hearing date for Friday, December 22, 1978. If successful at the hearing, Amirante would secure a temporary restraining order that would put a stop to the searches of Gacy's home, the surveillance, and the investigation.

On December 20, Gacy phoned Amirante several times. He had something to tell his attorney, and it was important. Amirante agreed to meet in his office, even though he had a sick son in the hospital and Christmas

BECOMING GACY'S LAWYER

Sam Amirante didn't know Gacy when the man first called. From Amirante's perspective, Gacy was an upstanding citizen and small-time politician who was being harassed by the police. To find out more, Amirante called Terry Sullivan, with whom he had worked on several cases. "He's a bad guy, a real bad guy," Sullivan said on the phone. "I can't tell you much, but I can tell you that."[5] Still, Amirante believed Gacy had just been in the wrong place at the wrong time and was being unjustly surveilled. Amirante agreed to take Gacy on as his client.

Amirante wrote the book *Defending a Monster* about his time serving as Gacy's lawyer.

shopping to do. For help, Amirante called in Leroy Stevens, another lawyer who had worked on business matters for Gacy. When their client arrived later that night, he appeared nervous and out of sorts. Gacy was not his usual confident self.

Then, Gacy let it all out. He confessed to kidnappings, assaults, and his involvement in the disappearance of Rob Piest. Gacy also described how he had strangled and murdered 20 or 30 young men and boys. By now, he couldn't be sure of the exact number. Gacy then dropped onto a couch in Amirante's office and fell asleep. "It was one of the scariest nights of my life," Amirante later told an interviewer. "My heart was pounding out of my chest."[6]

> **"I've been judge, jury, and executioner of many, many people."[7]**
>
> ***—John Wayne Gacy to Sam Amirante and Leroy Stevens***

The Arrest

When he arrived at work on Thursday, December 21, Lieutenant Kozenczak realized he had a problem. The hearing on Gacy's motion for a restraining order was scheduled for the next day. If the judge granted the order, the Gacy investigation would come to a halt. But Kozenczak was sure Gacy was responsible for Piest's disappearance. He had a little more than 24 hours to find solid evidence.

In the meantime, Terry Sullivan, a lawyer in the state attorney's office, began preparing a second search warrant. He relied on evidence already collected at

Gacy's house that linked Gacy to several missing boys. Sullivan had Kim Byers's statement that she had been wearing Rob Piest's jacket the night Rob disappeared, and she had pocketed the photo receipt that was later found in Gacy's house. Sullivan also had information from police officer John Schultz, who had been in Gacy's house and detected a foul smell coming from the crawl space. Michael Rossi and David Cram, two of Gacy's employees, had also testified. Rossi and Cram told investigators that Gacy had asked them to spread lime in the crawl space.

While Gacy snored on Amirante's office couch, the attorney called several Chicago hospitals, trying to get his client into a psychiatric unit. When Gacy woke, however, he had different ideas. He grabbed his coat and left with the police surveillance team, which had been sitting outside Amirante's office, on his tail.

To the cops, everything seemed routine, except for the fact that Amirante was now begging them not to lose Gacy. Amirante did not tell the cops why their surveillance had now become more urgent. Attorney-client privilege protected the confidential information Gacy had shared with his lawyer.

That morning and afternoon, Gacy drove wildly through the Chicago streets. In a rental car he was using

Before Gacy's arrest and while he was in custody, officers were concerned that Gacy might end his own life.

to replace the Oldsmobile seized by the police, he visited his father's grave. Later Gacy pulled into a Shell gas station where he knew the owner, John Lucas, and where PDM had its business account.

Lucas noticed that Gacy was quite upset, almost crying. At one point, Gacy pulled out a bag of marijuana, and handed it to Lance Jacobson, a juvenile standing inside the station. At first, Jacobson refused to take it. "Take it," Gacy said. "The end is coming. These guys are going to kill me."[8]

The police were watching as Jacobson handed the bag to Lucas. After Gacy left, officers entered the station and started asking questions. They confiscated the marijuana.

Meanwhile, Sullivan had a decision to make. He didn't have evidence yet to charge Gacy with murder, but he knew the upcoming hearing would put a stop to the investigation. While the Des Plaines police prepared another search warrant, Sullivan asked for updates from the two officers following Gacy.

Next Gacy drove to the house of a friend, Chris Gray. Nervous and depressed, Gacy confessed to Gray that he had admitted everything to his lawyers the night before. While Gacy was in the house, a new surveillance team arrived. The two officers spotted Gray and Gacy getting into Gacy's car and pulling away. The surveillance car followed.

The two cars then stopped at a restaurant. While Gacy was inside, Gray came up to the window of the unmarked police car. He told the waiting policemen that Gacy had just admitted to killing more than 30 people.[9] The officers immediately radioed this information to Sullivan.

A short time later, urgent instructions came down from Sullivan. Just after noon, at the intersection of Milwaukee and Oakton Avenues in the suburb of Niles, police officers arrested Gacy for possession of marijuana. He was driven to the Des Plaines station and put in a holding cell. The long chase was over.

Gacy had a mug shot taken the day after his arrest on December 21, 1978.

CHAPTER 8

DIGGING UP A NIGHTMARE

A few hours after Gacy's arrest on December 21, another team of police arrived at his home. For this second search, a much larger team had assembled. It included a Cook County evidence technician named Daniel Genty. His job was to search for any evidence of murder and any graves in or around the house.

By this time, the police had good reason to suspect Gacy had buried victims on his property. Officer Schultz had detected an odor coming from the crawl space. It smelled like decomposing bodies.

Genty had been in Gacy's house two years prior to this search. On that occasion, he had been searching for a missing girl. The girl was dating one of Gacy's employees, and Genty found the couple living with Gacy at West Summerdale Avenue. With the missing girl safely located, Genty had forgotten the incident until he found himself at Gacy's house once again.

Police spent many days thoroughly searching Gacy's home.

Now Genty headed for the closet trapdoor and the crawl space underneath. He found the crawl space flooded with water. There was a sump pump on the earthen floor. He turned it on, and the water began to drain.

Genty had a flashlight and a small shovel with him. When the sump pump had done its work and all the water had been drained from the crawl space, Genty dropped

Each body under Gacy's home was assigned a number while investigators worked to identify the victims.

to the floor, then walked a few feet and started digging. There were pools of water remaining in the earth, and Genty found clumps of hair in a few of them. Then his shovel struck something hard. Using his flashlight, Genty worked the earth with his gloved hand. He pulled up an arm bone.

"Charge him," Genty called up to Lieutenant Kozenczak, who was standing just above the crawl space. This was the evidence investigators needed. "I think this crawl space is full of kids," Genty remarked.[1] Remains from at least three bodies were found that evening before the search was called off for the day.

Making Statements

Gacy was already in police custody for possession of marijuana. On the night of December 21, he started talking to the police about the bodies found under his house. Gacy said the victims were drifters, street criminals, and hustlers who weren't worth all the trouble the police were making over them.

Over time, Gacy would offer many different responses to the charge of murder. He claimed to know nothing about the bodies, or he said that his PDM employees must be the real killers. He also blamed Jack Hanley for the killings. Jack Hanley was the identity Gacy had created while working at Bruno's.

Gacy had given similar excuses to Amirante, who was still serving as Gacy's lawyer. By talking so freely to the police, however, Gacy limited his attorney's options for a defense. There was no way to deny the confessions he had made. And there was no denying the bodies and other physical evidence that had turned up at his house.

"Please forgive me for what I am about to tell you. I have been very sick for a long time."[2]

—John Wayne Gacy in a letter to his family after his arrest

As Amirante saw it, Gacy had only one remaining defense to the charge of multiple homicides:

Gacy could plead insanity. This is a legal defense used to show that criminals have a significant mental illness that makes it impossible for them to know they are committing a crime. If Amirante could make a jury believe that this applied to Gacy, he might persuade them to find him not guilty by reason of insanity. This would mean his client would be committed to a psychiatric

Law enforcement later searched Gacy's mother's apartment building, looking for additional bodies. No human remains were found.

hospital rather than prison. Gacy would probably spend the rest of his life in confinement. But he would not be at risk of execution.

Confessions

In the meantime, Gacy had begun talking freely to the police. Lieutenant Kozenczak and other investigators found he was not shy about confessing to crimes he committed. In fact, he seemed to enjoy the attention. It became a pastime for him to chat with police who visited his cell. From these conversations, Gacy sensed that for once in his life he was considered somebody important.

Gacy also cooperated by assisting the police in the search for his victims. He drew a diagram of the crawl space, showing the exact locations of the 26 graves that he or his employees had dug.[3] He pointed out the spots where he had buried other victims, including under the

DEATH PENALTY IN ILLINOIS

The US Supreme Court struck down all death penalty laws in 1972, but Illinois's government worked to reinstate the death penalty. These efforts were upheld by the state Supreme Court in 1979, and the death penalty was reinstated in Illinois. However, its use was a controversial topic, and a debate raged in the state. In 2011, Illinois again abolished the death penalty. Between 1979 and 2011, 14 people were given lethal injections under the law in Illinois. In all, 362 people have been executed in the state's history, while 22 people have been freed from death row after being found innocent.[4]

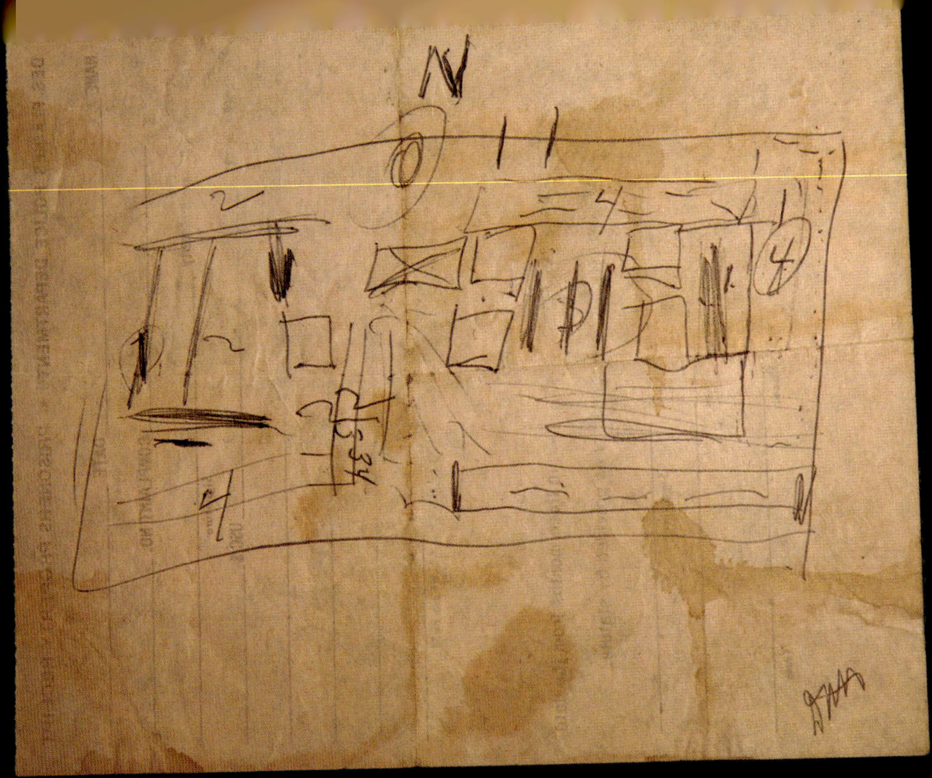

Gacy's diagram of burial locations on his property sped up the police's effort to locate victims' remains.

garage and in the backyard. One day, police drove Gacy to a bridge over the Des Plaines River, where Gacy admitted dumping four of his victims. At one end of the bridge, Gacy pointed out the spot where he had thrown the body of Rob Piest, his last victim, into the river.

A Media Frenzy

In all, 26 bodies were found in the crawl space of Gacy's home. Three bodies were found elsewhere on the property, and four were recovered from the Des Plaines River. The toll of known victims amounted to 33, making the killer clown the most prolific serial killer ever known at the time of his arrest.[5]

"He knew what he was doing . . . . He knew exactly where [the bodies] were."[6]

—Detective Michael Albrecht, discussing Gacy's diagram

News of the gruesome discovery spread through Chicago. A crowd of spectators and press gathered outside Gacy's home while a team of police dug up the buried remains. People stood in the January cold watching investigators go in and out Gacy's front door. Others jostled for a good view in the street or on the sidewalk. Some brought their families.

Officers covered each new body with a white sheet and placed it on a gurney. They wheeled each gurney outside to a waiting van. From time to time, the ambulance pulled away, headed for the Cook County medical examiner's office.

The search of Gacy's house became an international media event. Television news crews and print reporters from all over the world assembled on West Summerdale Avenue.

BURYING THE UNKNOWN

On June 13, 1981, the last of Gacy's victims were laid to rest. At this date, nine of the bodies recovered from his house and from the Des Plaines River were still not identified. But all were given an individual plot of ground in different cemeteries in the Chicago area, as well as a headstone inscribed with the words, "We Remembered."[7]

They interviewed residents, who spoke about the Gacy they knew and the goings-on at his home. Reporters tried to interview police and medical technicians, but everyone working on the case refused to talk outside of press conferences. In late December 1978 and the first weeks of 1979, news about Gacy became a constant feature in newspapers and on television. The media began calling him the Killer Clown.

THE GACY ROOM

Gacy's prolific crimes inspired a murder-themed room in a haunted house. Musician and filmmaker Rob Zombie opened a public Halloween attraction called Great American Nightmare in 2014. The haunted house was located in Villa Park, a Chicago suburb, and it included a Gacy Room. A live actor dressed up as Pogo the clown greeted visitors with balloons. Pogo stood near mannequins dressed as Boy Scouts, which were sitting on a sofa. The room became controversial for making light of Gacy's crimes. Terry Sullivan was interviewed about the Gacy Room. "I find it to be very despicable. I think it's cruel," he said.[8]

FORENSIC SPOTLIGHT

Using Teeth

Many of the bodies police found in Gacy's crawl space carried no easy means of identification. Since they were buried in the earth, decomposition advanced quickly. Their bodies, clothing, and faces had become unrecognizable. Specialists used forensic odontology, the science of using teeth to identify victims, to learn who was buried under Gacy's house.

Teeth are made of enamel and other hard materials that do not degrade after death. To help identify the victims, police turned to dental records. Potential victims' families provided dental records of the missing people. These records show the location of dental crowns and fillings, as well as any teeth that were damaged or missing. The dental records of missing people were compared to the teeth of the bodies uncovered at Gacy's house.

One of several victims identified in this way was John Szyc. The police found some of Szyc's possessions in Gacy's home, including a class ring and a television. But they could not positively identify Szyc as one of the victims until 1979, when they used records obtained from the Szycs' family dentist to confirm that his body was among those buried in Norwood Park.

Officers from the Cook County Sheriff's Department worked diligently to identify Gacy's victims.

CHAPTER 9

TRIAL AND EXECUTION

Murder trials often involve months of preparation by lawyers for both the prosecution and defense. These trials may also include several weeks of public hearings. In the most famous murder cases, the media and public pack courtrooms as the judge and jury make their decisions. And for cases of serial homicide, with the defendant possibly facing the death penalty, the entire process becomes more complicated.

Gacy's attorneys had an important job to do. It was up to them to defend their client's interests in court. Although Gacy's confessions were on record, he still had a

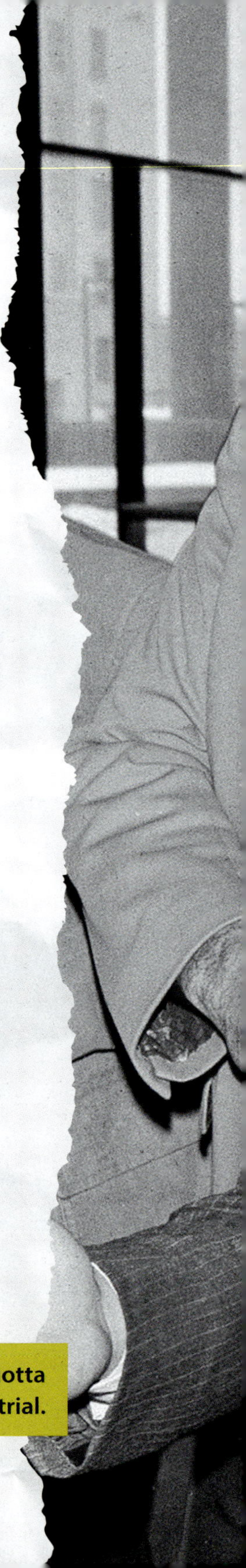

Amirante, *center*, was assisted by attorney Robert Motta in providing Gacy's legal defense during his trial.

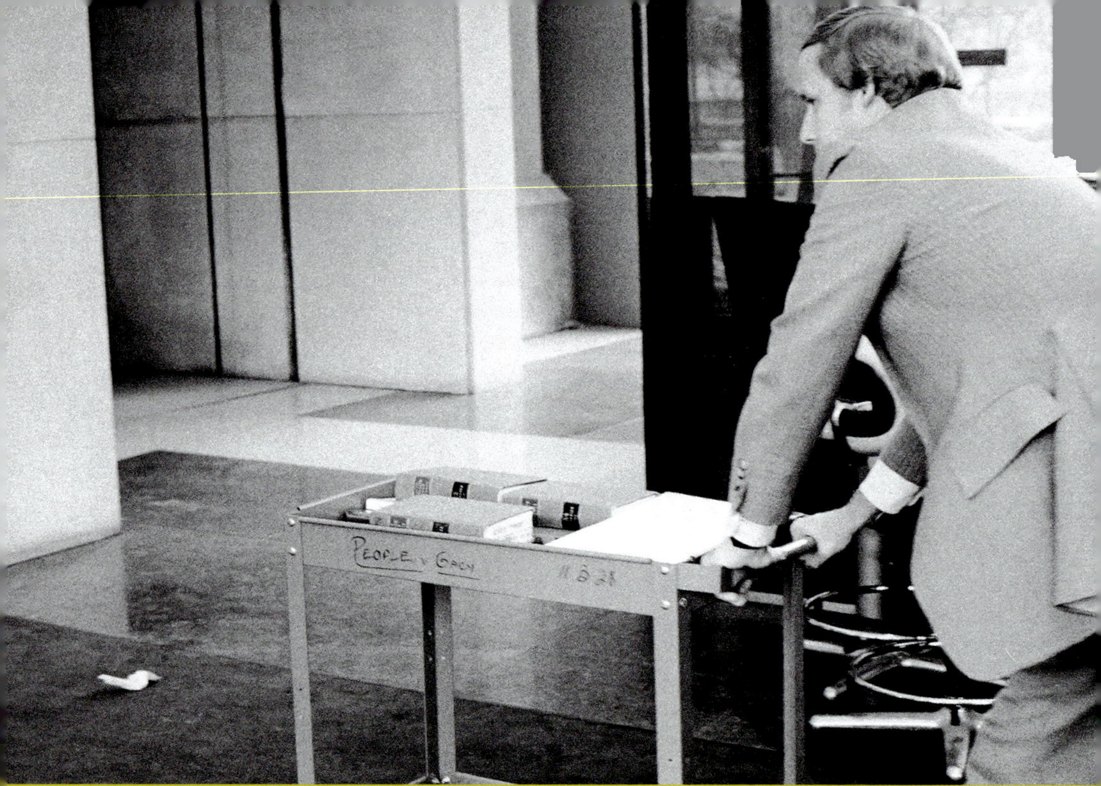

Terry Sullivan, *pictured*, spent many weeks preparing for Gacy's trial. He said the prosecution considered more than 100 people to give testimony as witnesses.

constitutional right to due process. This meant a public trial to determine his guilt or innocence, and what his sentence should be if he were found guilty.

Testing the Search Warrants

Lawyers for both sides have the right to file motions before a trial begins. One of the early motions in the Gacy case concerned the destruction of his house. The police and sheriff's office wanted to demolish the building to make the search for bodies easier. Gacy's lawyer opposed it. Sam Amirante said destroying the house would leave the defendant destitute. He argued the US Constitution barred the government from taking people's property without compensation. Amirante got a temporary stay, which postponed the demolition. But at a later hearing, his motion was denied. Gacy's house was destroyed in April 1979.

Gacy's lawyers also filed a motion to throw out the search warrant prepared by the Des Plaines police. They said police violated the law when they took the photo receipt from Gacy's home, as the receipt was not mentioned in the search warrant and was not reasonably tied to murder or any other crime at that time.

If the search warrant were thrown out, then evidence produced by the search could not be used in court, including the photo receipt, the class ring that linked Gacy to victim John Szyc, and other important items. It was likely, as a result, that Gacy would get a new trial. However, the motion to throw out the search warrant was also denied. The trial using this evidence would proceed.

Change of Venue

Gacy's trial was assigned to Judge Louis Garippo. His first responsibility was to handle the jury appointment. Each side had a right to contest the appointment of any jurors found to be biased. It would be difficult to find an unbiased jury in Cook County or Chicago, since Gacy's name was widely known. The case had been on the front page of every newspaper in the nation, and stories about the Killer Clown appeared in the *Chicago Tribune* and other local papers on a regular basis. Yet Gacy had a right to a jury of peers who were not likely to have prejudged his case.

BURNING THE CLOWNS

While he was in prison, Gacy turned to painting. He completed more than 2,000 canvases. Many depicted clowns, but Gacy also painted nature scenes, Elvis Presley, Adolf Hitler, the seven dwarfs from *Snow White*, and killers such as Ed Gein. After Gacy's death, some of his paintings were sold at auction. Joseph Roth and Walter Knoebel, two Chicago-area men, spent about $10,000 on Gacy's artwork in order to destroy it.[1] Relatives of Gacy's victims were present when Roth and Knoebel burned the paintings.

Before the trial began, Judge Garippo made a decision to move jury selection to Winnebago County, about 100 miles (160 km) west of Chicago. The city of Rockford, the Winnebago county seat, was large enough to provide an adequate pool of potential jurors. Garippo believed Rockford residents would be less familiar with Gacy's case and thus more likely to be unbiased. Once the jurors were selected, the trial itself would be held in Cook County, where Norwood Park and Chicago were located.

The jury for Gacy's trial was sequestered for seven weeks. This meant jury members were isolated and kept away from media during the trial to avoid becoming biased.

Pleading Insanity

Since Gacy had made multiple confessions to the police, the only defense he had left was insanity. If Gacy were found insane, he would be sentenced to an institution. But he would avoid the death penalty. To his own lawyer, there was no question that Gacy had been suffering from an intense mental illness when he committed his crimes. "I was convinced that this plea was not only his best and only course of action and in his best interest, it was absolutely true," Amirante said.[2]

Several of Gacy's unidentified victims were buried in separate cemeteries. Each has a headstone that says, "We Remembered."

Gacy's murder trial began in February 1980. The defense called upon several psychiatric experts during the trial to testify that Gacy was legally insane. Many of the psychiatrists who had interviewed Gacy diagnosed him differently. One psychiatrist believed Gacy experienced psychosis when he murdered his victims. While experiencing psychosis, a person can lose the ability to know what is real and what is fake. During an episode, someone may lose contact with reality, experience hallucinations, and hear voices.

Another possible explanation for Gacy's actions was that he had dissociative identity disorder (DID). People with DID may feel as though they have multiple personalities in their heads, which can lead to amnesia and a lack of control over one's actions. Gacy had told investigators that his mind was home to another personality, a police officer named Jack Hanley. Gacy claimed that Hanley committed the murders for which he was accused. Regardless of their diagnoses, doctors on the side of the defense agreed that Gacy did not have the mental capacity to act according to the law.

At Gacy's trial, prosecutors called the real James Hanley to the witness stand. They used Hanley to support their case. They wanted to show that Gacy's "Jack Hanley" persona was based on a real police officer, and was not just a figment of his imagination.

Prosecutors also had expert witnesses. They admitted that Gacy might have a mental illness. But they also suggested that he was faking his mental illness in order to get a lighter sentence and avoid the death penalty. He had attempted to evade detection, they argued, which was the action of a rational man. His careful burial of his victims under his own house showed a clear-minded attempt to hide evidence and avoid getting caught. These actions showed

> **"If I have to live in prison for the rest of my life, I'd rather be dead."[3]**
>
> ***—John Wayne Gacy in 1994***

Gacy covered his face as he walked into the courtroom in an attempt to avoid media attention.

Gacy knew what he had done was wrong, which meant that he had not been legally insane during his crimes.

"We've been waiting for this for 14 years, and when it's over with, it will be a relief."[4]

—Harold Piest, father of victim Rob Piest, in 1994

Final Witnesses

Several witnesses also testified as survivors with firsthand knowledge of Gacy's style of attack. Jeffrey Rignall, Donald Voorhees, and Robert Donnelly all spoke about Gacy's assaults and torture. Several of these witnesses were so shaken by their memories that they broke down on the stand and were unable to complete their testimony.

Gacy himself did not take the witness stand. During the trial, Gacy wrote a letter to the judge requesting a mistrial, claiming his lawyers were misrepresenting his wishes and were preventing him from testifying. Gacy said that his lawyers were using an insanity defense against his wishes. However, Judge Garippo denied the request, and the trial continued.

Closing arguments took place on March 11, 1980. During his closing argument, the defense counsel again asked Gacy be found not guilty by reason of insanity.

BRAIN STORIES

Dr. Helen Morrison is a psychiatrist whose specialty is studying the brains of serial killers. When Gacy was executed, Morrison was ready. She took part in the autopsy that was carried out on Gacy's body. She got permission from prison officials to leave the autopsy with Gacy's brain sealed in a jar.

Morrison was curious to find out if the brain had any abnormalities. She wondered if there was something in the shape or condition of the human brain that turned people into killers. She sent the brain to a medical examiner. The report stated that Gacy's brain was physically normal.

After deliberating for about two hours, the jury found Gacy guilty of sexual assault and 33 counts of murder.[5] The sentence was death. The execution was set for June 2, 1980.

Appeals and Execution

Yet Gacy would remain on Illinois's death row for the next 14 years. He took up painting while his attorneys filed appeals to hold off and reverse the death sentence. Studying law books in the prison library, Gacy also filed his own motions contesting the trial proceedings and outcome. One of the more significant appeals involved contesting the first search warrant. Gacy and his attorneys claimed this warrant was invalid due to its failure to state a crime. The appeals were denied.

In May 1994, Gacy's lawyers filed a last motion to the US Supreme Court for a stay of execution. This would have

Thousands of people gathered with signs, posters, and balloons to celebrate Gacy's execution.

stopped Gacy's execution until another appeal could be heard. But the high court rejected the motion.

On May 9, a crowd assembled in Daley Plaza in downtown Chicago to take part in what they called a Gacy Day Parade, celebrating his upcoming execution. Meanwhile, Gacy was moved by helicopter to Illinois's execution site at the Stateville Correctional Center. He was put to death shortly after midnight on May 10, 1994, by lethal injection.

Enduring Image

Despite presenting himself as a steward of his community, John Wayne Gacy carried out a second life that brought tragedy to those involved. Gacy ended the lives of at least 33 boys and young men, affecting countless others who were loved ones of his victims. Gacy remains one of the most prolific serial killers in history. He is also one of the most famous.

Academic, medical, and legal scholars research serial killers in an attempt to understand the psychology and motives that drive such horrific crimes. Whatever his motivations, and however his backstory contributed to his crimes, Gacy earned lasting notoriety. He has been the subject of many books, movies, and television documentaries that explore his life and crimes. Gacy's creepy clown image, seen in several famous photographs and in his paintings, also made him famous. Since his execution, the public fascination with Gacy's image as the Killer Clown has endured.

SHARING A LAST MEAL

The public fascination with Gacy and other US serial killers is strong throughout the world. One Japanese restaurant took advantage of this trend in 2018. Ningen, meaning "human restaurant," was a pop-up restaurant that remained open in Tokyo for just a couple of weeks. In many states, prisoners on death row choose their final meal before execution. Ningen recreated the last meals of famous prisoners. Gacy's selection appeared on the menu, including fried chicken and shrimp, french fries, and strawberries.

FORENSIC SPOTLIGHT

DNA Identification

Several of Gacy's victims whose bodies were found in late 1978 have still not been identified through 2024. But there may be a way to find out who they are. The DNA Doe Project is a nonprofit group that helped in the Gacy case. DNA is a chemical that contains unique genetic information. It can be used to identify victims of crimes and link people to their families and ancestors.

In 2021, investigators sent a DNA sample from one of Gacy's unidentified victims to a lab in Alabama for sequencing. This process uncovers unique patterns in a strand of DNA. The sequence was uploaded to GEDmatch, a service that uses DNA patterns to identify close relatives of the person from whom the DNA sample was taken.

The DNA Doe Project found that the sample was related to DNA taken from the mother and half brother of Francis Wayne Alexander, who went missing in Chicago in the 1970s. The group identified Alexander's remains more than 40 years after his body was found in John Wayne Gacy's crawl space. In the future, DNA technology could uncover the identities of other previously unknown victims.

The Cook County Sheriff's Department held a press conference in October 2021 to share the newly discovered identity of one of Gacy's victims, Francis Wayne Alexander.

ESSENTIAL FACTS

TIMELINE

Mar. 17, 1942: John Wayne Gacy is born to John and Marion Gacy in Chicago, Illinois.

1962: Gacy drives to Las Vegas, Nevada, where he gets work at Palm Mortuary.

Sept. 1964: Gacy marries his first wife, Marlynn Myers, in Springfield, Illinois.

Dec. 3, 1968: Gacy is convicted of sodomy in Waterloo, Iowa, and sentenced to ten years in an institution.

June 1970: Gacy is released on parole from Iowa's Anamosa State Reformatory and returns to Chicago.

Jan. 4, 1972: Gacy murders Timothy McCoy after picking him up at Chicago's Greyhound bus station the previous night.

Mar. 1976: Gacy divorces his second wife, Carole Hoff.

Dec. 30, 1977: Gacy picks up Robert Donnelly and forces him into the car at gunpoint. Gacy tortures Donnelly and then lets him go.

Dec. 21, 1978: Gacy is arrested for possession of marijuana. Soon after, police search his home and discover buried bodies.

Mar. 11, 1980: Gacy is convicted on 33 counts of murder and is sentenced to death.

May 10, 1994: Gacy is executed by lethal injection at the Stateville Correctional Center in Crest Hill, Illinois.

IMPACT ON SOCIETY

John Wayne Gacy was, for a time, the most prolific serial killer in US history, having been convicted of killing 33 people. Yet there was much more to his story than multiple homicides. Residents of Chicago questioned why Gacy's murder spree went undetected for almost seven years. Several victims had gone to the police after Gacy raped and tortured them, yet the police showed little or no interest in investigating these incidents.

The problem for many of Gacy's victims was not just their youth but also their lives on the margins of society. Eventually police took seriously the disappearance of his last victim, Rob Piest, the well-adjusted son of a stable, middle-class suburban family. It was the disappearance of Rob Piest that led directly to Gacy's investigation and arrest. The public became increasingly fascinated with Gacy's case during his trial and after his execution. The story of Gacy's life and crimes remains a popular subject for media, including movies and books.

QUOTE

"Clowns can get away with anything. . . . Clowns can get away with murder."

—*John Wayne Gacy*

GLOSSARY

alter ego

A separate personality that is acted out by a person, sometimes as the result of mental illness.

battery

A criminal offense involving physical contact.

chloroform

A chemical that can cause dizziness, drowsiness, and unconsciousness.

consensual

Involving the approval of everyone involved.

destitute

Lacking necessary resources or possessions.

embalm

To treat a dead body with chemicals to protect it from decay.

medical examiner

A doctor who works as a public officer and who determines cause of death.

mortuary

A business that handles the dead, preparing them for funerals and burial.

motion

A formal request for a desired ruling, order, or judgment in court.

parole

The supervised release of a prisoner before the full completion of their sentence, after which the person has to maintain good behavior for a certain period of time.

pedophile

A person who is sexually attracted to children.

probable cause

Evidence providing a reasonable basis for police to believe a crime has been committed.

prosecutor

A lawyer who leads the case against a defendant in court.

restraining order

A court order that bans certain actions, such as contact with or investigation of an individual.

sodomy

Anal or oral intercourse with another person, especially someone of the same sex.

stakeout

A police operation in which investigators watch a home or other location and the activities of a criminal suspect.

ADDITIONAL RESOURCES

SELECTED BIBLIOGRAPHY

Cahill, Tim. *Buried Dreams: Inside the Mind of Serial Killer John Wayne Gacy*. Bantam, 1986.

Nelson, David. *Boys Enter the House: The Victims of John Wayne Gacy and the Lives They Left Behind.* Chicago Review, 2022.

Sullivan, Terry. *Killer Clown: The John Wayne Gacy Murders.* Pinnacle, 2013.

FURTHER READINGS

Cummings, Judy Dodge. *Edmund Kemper: The Co-Ed Killer.* Abdo, 2025.

Lees, Amanda. *The True Crime Dictionary: From Alibi to Zodiac: The Ultimate Collection of Cold Cases, Serial Killers, and More*. Ulysses, 2021.

Rosewood, Jack. *The Ultimate Serial Killer Trivia Book: A Collection of Fascinating Facts and Disturbing Details about Infamous Serial Killers and Their Horrific Crimes.* LAK, 2022.

ONLINE RESOURCES

Booklinks
NONFICTION NETWORK
FREE! ONLINE NONFICTION RESOURCES

To learn more about serial killers, please visit **abdobooklinks.com** or scan this QR code. These links are routinely monitored and updated to provide the most current information available.

MORE INFORMATION

For more information on this subject, contact or visit the following organizations:

ANAMOSA STATE PENITENTIARY

406 N. High St.
Anamosa, IA 52205
doc.iowa.gov/find-facility/asp

John Wayne Gacy's first jail stay was from 1969 to 1970 at an institution now called the Anamosa State Penitentiary. It has a small museum that is open to visitors. Visitors can see a reconstruction of a cell, videos and photographs about the prison's history, and a gift shop.

CHICAGO HISTORY MUSEUM

1601 N. Clark St.
Chicago, IL 60614
chicagohistory.org

The Chicago History Museum displays a large collection of artifacts and exhibits showcasing the history of Chicago. Online digital resources include the True Crime LibGuide, with various holdings on the city's crime history.

NATIONAL CRIME MUSEUM

2757 Pkwy.
Pigeon Forge, TN 37863
alcatrazeast.com

Alcatraz East has a private museum that offers exhibits related to famous crimes and criminals. The museum's artifacts include a painting Gacy made of the seven dwarfs, painted on the side of a model semitruck.

SOURCE NOTES

CHAPTER 1. A MISSING PERSON

1. Courtney Lund O'Neil. "A Serial Killer, a Receipt, and My Mom: Haunted by the Murder of 33 Boys." *Harper's Bazaar*, 31 Oct. 2018, harpersbazaar.com. Accessed 10 June 2024.

2. Sam L. Amirante and Danny Broderick. *John Wayne Gacy: Defending a Monster.* E-book, Skyhorse, 2011.

3. Jerry Crimmins. "The Cops Who Closed In on John Wayne Gacy." *Chicago Tribune,* 24 Aug. 1980, newspapers.com. Accessed 25 Mar. 2024.

4. "People v. Gacy." *Justia US Law*, 6 June 1984, law.justia.com. Accessed 10 June 2024.

CHAPTER 2. GROWING UP GACY

1. Tim Cahill. *Buried Dreams: Inside the Mind of a Serial Killer.* Bantam, 1986. 22.

2. "John Wayne Gacy: 'The Dead Won't Bother You, It's the Living You Gotta Worry About.'" *YouTube*. Uploaded by True Crime Researcher, 30 Aug. 2022, youtube.com. Accessed 11 June 2024.

3. Christopher Berry-Dee and Steven Morris. *How to Make a Serial Killer: The Twisted Development of Innocent Children into the World's Most Sadistic Murderers*. Ulysses, 2008. 214.

CHAPTER 3. IN BUSINESS AND IMPRISONMENT

1. Juazel Pieterse. *John Wayne Gacy: A Psychobiographical Study.* 2012. Nelson Mandela Metropolitan University, MA thesis. *CORE*. 99.

2. "John Wayne Gacy." *Sioux City Journal*, 20 Mar. 2017, siouxcityjournal.com. Accessed 11 June 2024.

3. Donald H. J. Herman et al. "People of the State of Illinois vs. John Gacy: The Functioning of the Insanity Defense at the Limits of the Criminal Law." *West Virginia University*, vol. 86, no. 4, 1984, 1180, researchrepository.wvu.edu. Accessed 11 June 2024.

4. "The Life of the Party." *Conversations with a Killer: The John Wayne Gacy Tapes*, season 1, episode 1, Netflix, 20 Apr. 2022. *Netflix*, netflix.com. Accessed 11 June 2024.

CHAPTER 4. FIRST VICTIM

1. Donald H. J. Herman et al. "People of the State of Illinois vs. John Gacy: The Functioning of the Insanity Defense at the Limits of the Criminal Law." *West Virginia University*, vol. 86, no. 4, 1984, 1181, researchrepository.wvu.edu. Accessed 11 June 2024.

2. David Nelson. *Boys Enter the House: The Victims of John Wayne Gacy and the Lives They Left Behind*. E-book, Chicago Review, 2022.

CHAPTER 5. AN UPSTANDING CITIZEN

1. Colin McEvoy. "John Wayne Gacy." *Biography*, 16 June 2023, biography.com. Accessed 11 June 2024.

2. Courtney Lund O'Neil. "Remembering the 33 Victims of John Wayne Gacy." *Chicago Tribune*, 18 Dec. 2018, chicagotribune.com. Accessed 11 June 2024.

3. Richard Roeper. "John Wayne Gacy: The Never-Ending Aftermath of a Serial Killer's Notorious Crimes." *Chicago Sun-Times*, 19 Mar. 2021, chicago.suntimes.com. Accessed 11 June 2024.

CHAPTER 6. THE SUSPECT

1. "A Nicely Kept Secret." *Conversations with a Killer: The John Wayne Gacy Tapes*, season 1, episode 2, Netflix, 20 Apr. 2022. *Netflix*, netflix.com. Accessed 11 June 2024.

2. "A Nicely Kept Secret."

3. Kori Rumore and Kyle Bentle. "John Wayne Gacy's Victims: What Is Known about the 28 Identified and 5 Unknown Men." *Chicago Tribune*, 25 Oct. 2021, chicagotribune.com. Accessed 11 June 2024.

4. Terry Sullivan. *Killer Clown*. Pinnacle, 2013. 241.

SOURCE NOTES CONTINUED

CHAPTER 7. THE CHASE

1. David Nelson. *Boys Enter the House: The Victims of John Wayne Gacy and the Lives They Left Behind*. E-book, Chicago Review, 2022.

2. "Two Investigators: Were John Wayne Gacy Clown Suits Stolen from Evidence Room?" *CBS News*, 10 Feb. 2015, cbsnews.com. Accessed 11 June 2024.

3. Terry Sullivan. *Killer Clown*. Pinnacle, 2013. 41.

4. Sam L. Amirante and Danny Broderick. *John Wayne Gacy: Defending a Monster*. E-book, Skyhorse, 2011.

5. Amirante and Broderick, *John Wayne Gacy*.

6. "The Life of the Party." *Conversations with a Killer: The John Wayne Gacy Tapes*, season 1, episode 1, Netflix, 20 Apr. 2022. *Netflix*, netflix.com. Accessed 11 June 2024.

7. "The Life of the Party."

8. Sullivan, *Killer Clown*, 151.

9. Sullivan, *Killer Clown*, 153.

CHAPTER 8. DIGGING UP A NIGHTMARE

1. David Nelson. *Boys Enter the House: The Victims of John Wayne Gacy and the Lives They Left Behind*. E-book, Chicago Review, 2022.

2. Alec Wilkinson. "Conversations with a Killer." *New Yorker*, 10 Apr. 1994, newyorker.com. Accessed 11 June 2024.

3. Terry Sullivan. *Killer Clown*. Pinnacle, 2013. 193.

4. "History of the Death Penalty." *Death Penalty Information Center*, n.d., deathpenaltyinfo.org. Accessed 11 June 2024.

5. Donald H. J. Herman et al. "People of the State of Illinois vs. John Gacy: The Functioning of the Insanity Defense at the Limits of the Criminal Law." *West Virginia University*, vol. 86, no. 4, 1984, 57, researchrepository.wvu.edu. Accessed 11 June 2024.

6. Lauren Kranc. "Michael Albrecht Was There When John Wayne Gacy Confessed. He Saw through the Serial Killer's Charm." *Esquire*, 25 Mar. 2021, esquire.com. Accessed 11 June 2024.

7. "John Wayne Gacy Victims Remembered on 40th Anniversary of Arrest." *ABC7*, 21 Dec. 2018, abc7chicago.com. Accessed 11 June 2024.

8. Kim Bellware. "Haunted House with 'John Wayne Gacy Room' Erected near Where Serial Killer Was Active." *Huffington Post*, 17 Oct. 2014, huffpost.com. Accessed 11 June 2024.

CHAPTER 9. TRIAL AND EXECUTION

1. "John Wayne Gacy's Victims' Relatives Destroyed His Artwork in a Huge Bonfire." *Sinister Isles*, n.d., sinisterisles.com. Accessed 11 June 2024.

2. Sam L. Amirante and Danny Broderick. *John Wayne Gacy: Defending a Monster*. E-book, Skyhorse, 2011.

3. "Growing Up with John Wayne Gacy." *Oprah*, 17 Feb. 2010, oprah.com. Accessed 11 June 2024.

4. Lindsey Tanner. "Killer Gacy Is Executed in Illinois." *Greensboro News & Record*, 9 May 1994, greensboro.com. Accessed 11 June 2024.

5. Amirante and Broderick, *John Wayne Gacy*.

INDEX

ABOUT THE AUTHOR

TOM STREISSGUTH

Tom Streissguth is the author of more than 150 books of history, biography, and media studies for young people. He is a graduate of Yale University, where he majored in music, and has worked as a teacher and book editor. His website *The Archive of American Journalism,* which collects nonfiction articles from more than a dozen renowned American writers, has become an important resource for students and authors.